DAVID
ROBINSON

Books in the Today's Heroes Series

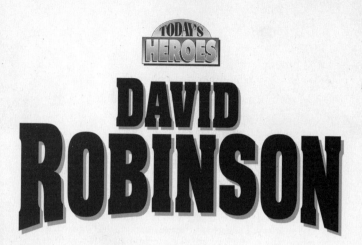

DAVID ROBINSON

by Steve Hubbard

ZondervanPublishingHouse

Grand Rapids, Michigan

A Division of HarperCollinsPublishers

David Robinson
Copyright © 1996 by Ambrose Robinson

Requests for information should be addressed to:

📕 ZondervanPublishingHouse
Grand Rapids, Michigan 49530

Library of Congress Cataloging-in-Publication Data

Hubbard, Steve
    David Robinson.
       p. cm. — (Today's heroes)
    Abridged version of How to raise an MVP.
    Summary: Focuses on the personal life and Christian
upbringing of the basketball star who played for the Naval
Academy and the 1988 Olympic team before becoming center
for the San Antonio Spurs.
    ISBN: 0-310-20906-4
    1. Robinson, David, 1965–   —Juvenile literature.
2. Basketball players—United States—Biography—Juvenile
literature.   3. Basketball players—United States—Religious
life—Juvenile literature.   [1. Robinson, David, 1965– .
2. Basketball players.   3. Afro-Americans—Biography.   4.
Christian life.]   I. Hubbard, Steve (Steve A.) How to raise an
MVP.   III. Title.   IV. Series.
GV884.R615R63   1996
796.323'092—dc20
  [B]   96-11122
                                                   CIP
                                                       AC

Illustrations by Gloria Oostema
Printed in the United States of America

00 01 02 /❖ DH/ 10 9

Contents

Chronology of Events

August 1965. David Maurice Robinson is born.

1982–83. David plays high school basketball for the first time as an Osbourne Park senior. He scores 1320 on his SATs and is accepted to the Naval Academy at 6'7$\frac{1}{2}$".

1983–84. David grows to 6'9" by the time school starts and becomes the Midshipmen's backup center as Navy wins twenty games for the first time in the school's history.

1984–85. David begins his second season as a 6'11" starter and ends it as a 7'1" sophomore star. Navy goes 26–6 and makes the NCAA playoffs for the first time since 1966.

1985. After long discussions with his parents, David decides to stay at Navy even though it means he might have to spend five years in the military after college.

1985–86. David becomes an All-American as a

junior and leads Navy to within one victory of the Final Four.

1986–87. David repeats as an All-American, sets thirty-three Navy records, and is named College Player of the Year.

1987. Navy Secretary James Webb says David must serve two years in the Navy after graduation and won't be able to play in the NBA during that time.

May 1987. David graduates from Navy and is commissioned an ensign in the Naval Reserve. Three days later, the San Antonio Spurs win the first pick in the NBA lottery and say they will select David in the June draft despite his military commitment.

September 1987. David visits San Antonio, which begins to convince him he can turn around the Spurs the same way he did the Midshipmen.

November 1987. David signs a $26 million contract.

September 1988. David starts in the Olympics, but the United States finishes only third and David averages only 12.8 points and 6.8 rebounds.

November 1989. David makes his NBA debut and leads the Spurs to victory over the fabled Los Angeles Lakers.

1990. David is named an All-Star and NBA Rookie of the Year.

1991. David wins the NBA rebounding title.

June 1991. David becomes a born-again Christian.

December 1991. David marries Valerie Hoggatt.

1992. David is named NBA Defensive Player of the Year and wins the blocked shot title.

August 1992. David leads the U.S. Dream Team to the gold medal in the Olympics.

January 1993. David's first child, David Jr., is born.

1994. David wins his first NBA scoring championship.

April 1995. David's second child, Corey Matthew, is born.

1995. David is named NBA MVP and becomes the first male basketball player selected to three U.S. Olympics teams.

1996. David is named to his seventh straight All-Star Game.

1

The Miracle

Long before he could run and dunk and block shots like no other player in basketball—why, before he could even walk—David Robinson nearly died.

It was February 1966, and the Robinsons were living in Newport, Rhode Island. David was six months old and a fat little baby boy. He had a sister, Kimberly, who was almost three, and a mom named Freda and a dad named Ambrose.

Mr. Robinson's job was handling sonar, a form of radar that locates things underwater for big Navy ships when they go out to sea. Sometimes they would be gone for months at a time. This was one of those times. The *U.S.S. Van Voorhis* was leaving for South America.

Freda Robinson thought this would be a good time to visit her sister, Jessie Mitchell, in Rye Beach, New Hampshire. Jessie lived only a couple of hours away, but the weatherman had predicted a big ice storm, so David's dad had warned his mom to stay home.

She didn't listen. She dropped off her husband at the ship, packed up the car and kids, and left for Rye Beach. They arrived with no problem, but a couple of days later, the icestorm hit. The roads were too slippery to drive. School was canceled. Everybody was told to stay home unless going out was an absolute emergency.

David woke up crying. His mom lifted him out of his portable crib, gave him a big hug, and rested him on the bed while she went to the kitchen for his bottle. While she waited for the milk to warm up, David stopped crying, and she figured he had fallen back asleep. So Mrs. Robinson talked with her sister for a few minutes before checking in on David.

She looked in the room—David wasn't on the bed. He wasn't on the floor. Where was he? She figured Jessie's husband must have scooped him up and taken him to his room to play.

She knocked on his door and said, "Mitch, do you have David?"

"No, I don't," he said.

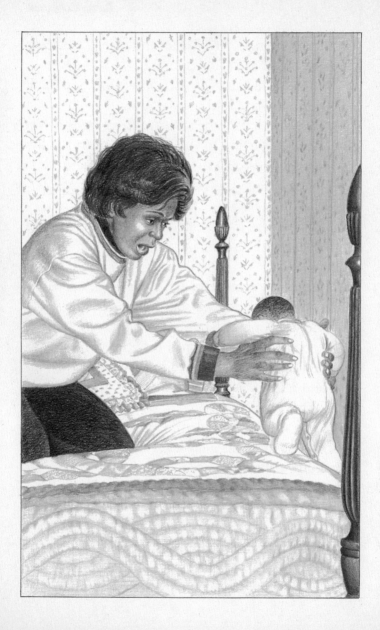

"Don't kid me," Mrs. Robinson replied. "He needs his bottle, and I can't find him."

Mitch came out in his house coat and said, "Freda, I don't have him."

"You're serious?" she said. "Well, where *is* he?"

She was starting to worry. She went in the living room and asked all the kids, "Is David here?"

"No, ma'am," they said, and now she was getting scared.

"Well, where *is* he?" she asked, and she scurried back to David's bedroom and started looking all over again.

Finally, she spotted the top of his head, just barely sticking out above the side of the bed. David was too young to walk or crawl, but he had rolled off the edge of the bed and gotten trapped between the mattress and the wall. He was jammed in there so tightly, his nose and mouth were mashed against the mattress. He couldn't breathe.

She ran and picked him up. He had stopped breathing so long, his body had turned blue. She was scared. She panicked.

"He's dead!" she screamed. "My baby is dead!"

Her sister ran into the room and said, "Stop it! Look, he *will* be dead if you don't give him CPR."

Mrs. Robinson was a nurse. She knew people can go only four to six minutes without breathing before they suffer brain damage. She knew a few minutes more than that, and they can't live at all. She knew how to perform artificial respiration and CPR (cardiopulmonary resuscitation) to bring breathing and heart beating back to normal. But she'd only practiced on plastic dummies.

"I've never done it on a human!" she wailed. "I've only done it on a mannequin! I can't do it on him!"

"If you don't want him to die," her sister said, "you better try."

Still scared but realizing she needed to act quickly, Mrs. Robinson laid David on his back on the bed. She opened his mouth and ran her fingers inside to make sure nothing was stuck in his throat. She put her ear to his chest and couldn't feel or hear him breathing. She tipped his head back, placed her mouth over his mouth and nose, and blew air into his mouth and down his lungs. She waited three seconds and blew again.

Mrs. Robinson had gone to church for as long as she could remember. She believed in the power of God. And now she called upon him. "Lord," she said, screaming and praying at the same time, "don't let my child die!"

She breathed into David's mouth a third time and then a fourth.

She thought she saw David's chest move.

So did her sister. "It looks like he's breathing!" Jessie shouted.

He was!

Mitch hung up the phone and assured everyone

that an ambulance was on the way. But the scare wasn't over. David's little eyes started rolling back in his head as if he had no control, and his mom was afraid he was going into convulsions. She thought quickly. Maybe the cold winter air would shock him out of the convulsion. Freda Robinson scooped up her baby, ran out of the bedroom, through the kitchen, and into the garage. Out in the cold air, David's eyes stopped rolling. His body grew cold, and he began to cry.

His mom wrapped him in blankets, trying to get his temperature back to normal. Finally, the ambulance arrived. The paramedics had been slowed by the slippery roads. When they came into the house, they asked where the sick baby was.

"This is the baby," David's mom said, nodding to the baby in her arms.

They looked at David and couldn't believe this was the same baby who had been blue and not breathing.

"Whatever you did must have worked," they said. "He's just cold now."

They carried him out to the ambulance and took him to the hospital. The doctors and nurses helped get his body temperature back to normal and sent David to a nearby military hospital for the night.

The doctors wanted to know how long David had gone without oxygen, and his mom told them she didn't know. Had he stopped breathing as soon as he stopped crying, or some time after that? She had no way of knowing. She figured she'd been gone at least five minutes, probably more, but she didn't know how much of that time David had gone without breathing.

Without knowing that, the doctors said they wouldn't be able to tell for years whether David had suffered brain damage.

"You mean I'll have to wait until he starts learning or talking?" his mom asked.

"That's about the size of it," the doctors replied.

That scared her.

But the scares still weren't over.

Two days later, her sister wanted to go shopping, so Mrs. Robinson bundled her children in their warmest clothes. Kimberly and Jessie jumped into the back seat. David lay loose on the front seat, next to his mom. There were no car seats for babies then.

The roads were still sheets of ice. As they went through an intersection, another lady's car couldn't stop on the ice. It slid toward them.

Bam!

It crashed right into the passenger's side of the Robinsons' car. David's side! David was unprotected. Somehow, he didn't get hurt. His mom and sister and aunt were okay, too.

But one whole side of the car was torn up, and Ambrose Robinson had always been very fussy about his car. He had warned his wife not to drive in this weather, and she had ignored him. Now she had wrecked his car and put his children in danger, and her carelessness in leaving a baby on a big bed had caused David who-knows-what harm.

Freda Robinson knew she had to tell her husband the news, and she was a nervous wreck because she knew he'd be furious. She couldn't even call to tell him because he was somewhere in the middle of the Atlantic Ocean. All she could do was write him a letter, call Red Cross, and wait and worry.

She knew she'd made mistakes. She felt so bad about them that she didn't need her husband to holler and scream "I told you so."

Finally, David's dad got the message and was able to phone home.

"Are you hurt? Is David hurt? Did Jessie get hurt?" he asked.

"Nobody got hurt," Mrs. Robinson said. "The car is just destroyed."

"I'm so glad none of you got hurt," he said. He didn't complain at all about his car. He knew it was not the time to criticize, but inside, he was upset by the auto accident and frightened by his son's condition.

They were going to have to live with the fear and guilt about whether David's mind had been slowed.

2

The Blessing

It was a daily ritual when David was three. Every morning, Mrs. Robinson would tell her children, "The Dr. Seuss show is coming on TV!"

David and Kimberly would run to get their Dr. Seuss books. They owned just about every one. Then they'd pull up their little chairs and plop in front of the TV. The host would tell them the book of the day, and they'd find the right one and open it up. Then they'd read along with the host and follow the action on the screen and in the book. If David couldn't read a word, the host or his big sister would help him out.

Still, David's parents didn't know if he could really read words or if he was just reading the pictures.

Then one day the Robinsons were leaving Key West, Florida, driving north on U.S. Highway 1.

David stood on the back seat and peered over his father's shoulder.

"Daddy, you're speeding," he said.

"No, I'm not," his father fibbed.

David pointed to the sign along the side of the road.

"SPEED LIMIT 55," it said.

He pointed to the odometer on the dashboard in front of his daddy.

"You're going sixty, and the speed limit is fifty-five," he said.

His parents looked at each other as though to say, "Can you believe this?"

Their little boy was only three, and he could already read!

He could read more than just pictures. He could read numbers. He could read words and whole sentences.

His brain wasn't scarred! He was smarter than almost every kid his age!

His parents were excited and relieved.

For three anxious, awful years, they had wondered if the accident had harmed him. Now their worries were over. David's mom thanked the Lord and counted her blessings. She considered it a miracle.

Freda and Ambrose Robinson decided God must have saved their little boy's life for a special reason. For what reason, they weren't yet sure, but they were about to find out.

3

Early Lessons

David's parents always preached about the importance of education. And he could tell they meant it because they didn't just talk about it, they did something about it.

They read to Kimberly and David and later to baby brother Chuck, who was born six years after David. They bought flash cards and quizzed their children on letters and words and numbers. They made reading and learning into a game. They liked to travel, and whenever they did, they'd ask the kids to read road signs, license plates, and the model of cars they were passing.

They bought educational toys. They set up an area

in the house for learning. They had a chalkboard to use to teach, a bulletin board to put up little notes, and a yardstick to point to things and show them how to measure. They watched TV shows the children could learn from, such as *Jeopardy* and *Name That Tune*. They watched football, baseball, and basketball on TV too, but they always emphasized books more than balls.

"If you can make it in sports, great," Mr. Robinson told David. "But not many people do, and most likely, you'll need to fall back on your education. Without an education, you can't do anything. With a proper education, you can do anything you want to do."

Pushed by his parents, David discovered he liked to learn. He was quick to learn, too. He knew his lessons so well in second grade that he kept finishing ahead of everyone else. Then he'd start talking and bothering the other kids. Finally, the principal called his parents to the office and recommended moving David ahead to third grade.

"I do not want him skipped," his dad said.

"I want you to give him more advanced work to keep him busy," his mom said. "Keep giving him more advanced work until he stops being able to finish."

And that's what they did until the next school year when Virginia Beach started a new program for gifted children. Even in a class with the city's smartest kids, David continued to excel.

David was good at math. That came in handy

because the Robinsons were a middle-class family and had to watch how much money they spent. His mom made out a grocery list and walked across a little bridge with David to a grocery store called the Lion. David kept track of how much money she spent, and he knew the exact total before they got to the checkout counter. If she didn't have enough money, he'd tell her what items to put back. He'd also divide the cost per ounce of, say, different jars of peanut butter to tell her which was the better bargain. This was when David was in third or fourth grade and few people owned calculators. No matter. David's mom said she had a "human calculator."

David also loved to read, and he especially loved science fiction. He devoured the books as quickly as he could get them. Once in fifth grade, he begged his mom for one particular book. She finally told him she would buy it for him on Saturday when she had the day off and was going shopping with his godmother.

When they got to the bookstore, David discovered the exact book he wanted—along with all the other books in its series.

"Geeeee!" he squealed. "All five right here! Mom, can you buy them all?"

"No," his mom said. "You said you wanted one book, and I've only got seven dollars with me."

"Mom," he replied, "don't you have a charge card? Put it on that!"

"He's right," David's godmother chimed in. "Put it

on your charge card. You put everything else you want on it. If my kids would read like David, I would buy the whole library and bring it home."

His mom was outnumbered. Her husband felt the same way, too: If a child wants a book, buy it. He figured you could spoil children with too many toys, but you could never spoil them with too many books. He thought books were the best way to learn. So the Robinsons bought fun books such as Dr. Seuss and science fiction. They bought educational books such as *The Guinness Book of World Records* and magazines like *Highlights for Children*.

If the kids asked their mom what a word meant, she'd say, "Get the dictionary. You'll remember it better if you look it up." If they said they were bored, their dad told them to read a book or else he'd give them a chore to do. If they said they had nothing to read, he'd tell them to pick up the dictionary and learn new words.

The more David read, the more he loved it. When everybody else was out playing sports, David would be sitting reading a book. Kids his age thought he was a reading nerd, a bookworm.

When he was supposed to be in bed, fast asleep, his dad would check on him, and he'd be under the covers, reading with a flashlight. That happened so often that once, when the electric power went out, his mom went straight to David's room.

She knew she could always find a flashlight there.

4

Dad School

David Robinson stood, staring as his father fixed the family car. Dad dazzled David. Other kids found their heroes in sports or music or movies. David found his hero in the driveway, the living room, the backyard—in his own father.

Mr. Robinson played Beethoven's "Moonlight Sonata" on the piano. He put together radios and TVs out of tiny electronics kits. He taught David how to hit a baseball from both sides of the plate, how to dribble a basketball, how to hit a bull's-eye with his bow and arrow, how to roll strikes at the bowling alley, and how to choose the right bait for each species of fish. And now here he was, sliding under the car, solving yet another problem.

David was ten or twelve, a smart kid, but he couldn't understand all this.

Man, he thought, how can one man have a general knowledge of everything?

Finally, he spoke up.

"Did you go to Dad School or something?" he asked.

No, he did not. But Ambrose Robinson could be the father of Dad Schools all around the country. He taught David how to be the National Basketball Association's Most Valuable Player—and a Most Valuable Person, too.

Long before David grew to be 7'1" and an All-Star center for the San Antonio Spurs, his dad taught him to excel in many subjects.

David learned about so many interests, he amazes people today as much as his father amazed him when he was young. "How are you good at everything?" they ask him. "You play in the NBA, you're a good bowler and golfer, you do gymnastics, you play Ping-Pong, you play the piano and saxophone, you got a math degree from Navy, you know computers, you do this, you do that. How in the world can you do everything?"

"I got it from Dad," he replies. "Dad was into everything."

Take the piano, for instance. As a toddler, David listened to his dad play, then climbed on the seat and banged away on the piano keys. But his dad didn't want to listen to racket, so he taught David about notes. Gradually, David began to put the notes together and play parts of songs. He had a great gift of listening to a song and then playing it by ear, without even seeing the sheets of music in front of him. One of the first songs he played was his dad's favorite, "Moonlight Sonata," even though it is a difficult classical piece. Later, his father taught him to read music off the same sheet music he had studied as a child.

David also copied his father's love of math, engineering, and electronics. David became so good in math that his teacher would drive to the Robinson house, drop off the students' tests, and let David grade them. Once the instructor forgot to leave the answer sheet.

David called and told him, and the teacher simply said, "That's fine. You already know the answers. You don't need the master sheet."

And he didn't.

Mr. Robinson liked to tear apart things to see how they worked or why they didn't work anymore. He would buy something that cost $400 or $500—a lot of money in those days—and would work or play with it for a while and then put it aside and go to something else. It didn't hold his interest anymore. It wasn't challenging enough.

David inherited that same curiosity. He was never afraid to try something new. His parents told him he could do anything if he set his mind to it and worked at it.

"There are no such words as 'I can't' in my household," Mr. Robinson told David.

And his mom said, "A lot of people will say, 'I can't do that.' Oh, yes, you can!"

Mr. Robinson taught David how to use the TV and stereo before he even started school. He showed his son how to make TVs and radios from kits before he finished elementary school. David knew the difference between a transistor, a diode, and a capacitor when he was still in elementary school. He knew the names of all kinds of tools and how to use them.

A few years later, this knowledge would lead to one of his most impressive feats.

5

Stealing Candy

David looked up and down the aisle at the 7-Eleven. No one was looking except his four-year-old brother. He slid the candy bar inside his clothes and left without paying.

It's not really stealing, the ten-year-old thought. It's just a little five-cent candy bar. This big old store won't miss it.

When David and Chuck got home, David started eating the candy and Chuck started hollering because he wanted a piece. Their dad heard the ruckus and wondered where they got the candy.

"We got it from the store," Chuck said.

"You didn't have any money to pay for it," their dad said.

"David took the candy," Chuck said.

That was all Mr. Robinson had to hear. He would not tolerate shoplifting in his home. He loaded both boys in his car, drove back to the store, and made David walk up to the cashier.

David looked around the store. His neighbors and friends were watching. He stared at the floor. He was so embarrassed and nervous, he started crying.

"I want to apologize," he said. "I stole this candy bar."

The cashier said, "Well, you can have it since you were honest enough to tell me."

The father said, "No, he cannot have it. It is not his candy."

And then Mr. Robinson took his boys home and spanked them both with his belt. David was spanked for stealing. Chuck was spanked for going along with the crime.

That was the first and last time any Robinson took what didn't belong to him. It didn't matter if it were as expensive as a car or as cheap as a two-cent piece of candy. Stealing was stealing, and stealing was wrong.

Stealing, cheating, and lying broke all the Robinson Rules. Honesty was especially important to Mr. Robinson because he didn't want his children to repeat the same mistakes he had made as a teenager.

He had broken into homes and stolen things. He had signed a neighbor lady's check to pay for a Ping-Pong table and had gotten caught. He could have been sent to jail for that, but the lady didn't have him arrested because she knew his parents were good church people. If she hadn't been nice, he would have been sent to reform school, the same reform school where, a short time later, a big fire had broken out, killing eighty-five boys. Ambrose Robinson could have been one of them.

Still, he did not learn his lesson. When he went away to college, he broke into some other students' lockers and was caught drinking alcohol, which was against county law. He was kicked out of college and sent home in disgrace.

"You'll never be anything!" his father had screamed at him.

I'm gonna show you, Ambrose Robinson decided, and he did. He joined the Navy, worked hard, and climbed the ranks to senior chief, the second-highest rank an enlisted man can achieve. He married Freda Hayes and they had three lovely children. He vowed to correct them quickly if he saw them repeating the mistakes he had made. He would not allow them to steal. He would not allow them to lie. He would not take his children to the movies and lie about their ages just to get a cheaper ticket.

Mr. and Mrs. Robinson told their children that

character and honesty were more important than even ability. They demanded their children display upstanding character, and they disciplined them when they didn't. They might be spanked. They might be restricted to their room, house, or yard. They might lose part or all of their allowances. They might lose other privileges, such as attending a movie or a fun event.

David thought his parents were ogres.

They're so strict, he told himself, it's ridiculous. My friends aren't put on restriction for a bad grade. They can say all kinds of stuff to their parents and not get spankings. Dad's been in the military too long. He needs to get out. Real people aren't like this.

He didn't realize that loving discipline is what every kid needs.

His parents were especially tough when it came to grades. If David didn't bring home work, his parents made up some for him to do. His mom checked out his homework before he started, and his father reviewed his answers before he was allowed to go out and play. And if Mr. Robinson did not approve, watch out!

Once, David brought home a report card that would make most parents proud: an A, two B's, and a C.

And he got grounded for six weeks!

The C was in one of his best subjects, but he had a problem with the teacher. Mr. Robinson, however, wouldn't take any excuses. Until David boosted that C the next time grades came out, he could not leave his house or yard to play with his friends after school.

David was so bright, he could get up an hour early, dash off an assignment, and still get a better grade than almost everyone in his class. He knew he could get by in school without studying hard, and so he didn't. He was lazy. But his parents held him to a higher standard than his teachers did. They wouldn't let him coast.

"If you make an A and could have made an A-plus, you might as well have made an F because you haven't given your all," his mom told him.

His parents were also big on responsibility and religion.

In grade school, David, Kimberly, and Chuck all had their own chores. Chuck was mowing the lawn before he was tall enough to see over the mower's handle. Detailed instructions for all the children were posted every day on the refrigerator or on the bulletin board. David and Chuck often cooked. Kimberly washed dishes. All three took turns vacuuming, scrubbing, and tidying up not only their bedrooms but the whole house. The boys mowed the lawn, trimmed the shrubs, took out the garbage, cleaned the garage, washed the car, split firewood, and brought it inside.

Chores helped teach David about responsibility.

Church helped teach him about right and wrong.

Mrs. Robinson didn't just send her children to

church; she took them with her. When they were babies, they stayed in the nursery, but when they turned two or three, they sat in church beside her. She didn't want them playing in the nursery anymore. She knew they wouldn't understand it all and she knew they wouldn't always sit still and listen. But she wanted them to pay their respects to God and to start to learn about religion.

Most of the time, the children liked church. They had lots of fun activities, and they got to meet other kids and go on special church outings.

But they noticed their dad didn't go to church all the time.

"Dad's not going," they said once. "Why do we have to?"

Their dad did not have a good answer. Their mom did not, either. If going to church were so important for the kids, why wasn't it important for Dad? If he didn't practice what he preached, why should they?

Mrs. Robinson thought about it.

She prayed about it.

The next time they asked, she had an answer. She said, "You owe it to the Lord. He's been good to you this week."

And she said, "I want you to give God praise for what he has done for you, and you might learn something you don't already know. We all need the Lord, and I ask very little of you, but this is one thing I'm asking you to do. I'm not sending you; I'm taking you with me. One or two hours is not that long."

Her children frowned.

"We don't want to go," they said, "but if you want us to go, we will."

Even when they became teenagers, she did not give them a choice. She gave them the freedom to make many decisions on their own, but this one was not negotiable. They would go to church every Sunday as long as they lived in her home.

She insisted they pray and attend church. She told them prayer and church attendance might not seem important now, but they would find it meant a great deal when they were older. David didn't really understand.

He blessed his food before every meal and said his prayers every night. He believed in God. Often, he would say, "Without God, this wouldn't happen." He respected the values of the church. But he didn't really think about God when he wasn't in church. David thought the stories about Jesus were like fairy tales. They were neat stories, the same kind he read in the history books about George Washington.

God would not be the guiding force in David's life for several years.

6

Sports Success— and Failure

David tossed open the front door, ran into the kitchen to find his mom, and sounded an imaginary trumpet.

"Da-daaa-DAAAAAH!" he said and spread three or four first-place blue ribbons on the kitchen table for his mom to admire.

This was a scene repeated often throughout grade school. Even though David was a little nerdy, sports came as easily as school. The brain child competed in just about everything and won just about everything.

One time, when he was nine or ten, he won the

Virginia long jump competition. That meant David and his coach would drive to Kentucky to compete in the national championships.

He finished second—but he knew he would have won if he hadn't fallen.

When he came home and his mom picked him up, he had a long face.

Mrs. Robinson had talked to the coach on the phone. She knew what had happened, and she was proud her boy had finished second in the whole country.

"David, where's your ribbon?" she asked in a really soft voice.

"Mom," he said, his voice sad as could be, "I didn't want to show it to you. I only won the red."

That was David. He always set high goals for himself. And he usually achieved them.

When he was nine or ten and played community-league baseball, he could do it all. He could run. He could throw. He could hit. Every time he came to bat, the people in the stands would bet on whether he'd hit a home run. And quite often he did, either right-handed or left-handed.

When he was eleven, his father took him to a golf course for his first golf lesson. It was awkward at first. Mr. Robinson was about a foot taller than David, and his clubs were way too long. Plus, they were made for a right-hander, and David is left-handed.

Didn't matter.

David went around the course, and with his dad telling him what club to use and how to hit it, he shot about a 124 and won the tournament for his age group.

First time he ever played golf—and he won!

David and Chuck were good in gymnastics, too. They could tumble and flip over the hedges in their front lawn—and the hedges were four feet high! David could walk across the floor or the lawn on his hands.

David's dad had been an excellent athlete himself. He might have played pro basketball, except in those days, blacks were rarely allowed to play. He was only in his early twenties when his first two children were born, and he was like an overgrown kid who loved to play right alongside them. He took the family fishing and bowling. He showed the boys how to hit baseballs and throw footballs and shoot basketballs. He taught his children archery and gymnastics, and he taught a whole group of neighborhood kids how to bowl. He was an assistant coach in Little League baseball and in pee-wee football.

When he wasn't coaching the kids' organized games, he was watching from the stands. When they weren't playing sports, they'd gather around the TV and watch the pro and college games. They loved the Miami Dolphins. They watched the World Series and the Final Four. They watched the NBA playoffs, especially when their favorites, the Boston Celtics and Los Angeles Lakers, were playing.

Mr. Robinson taught them enough about each sport that if they wanted to play, they knew how. He taught them to try hard to win against everybody from their siblings to other schools in everything from Monopoly to bowling. Competition, he told them, brought out the best in everyone.

But while David's dad enjoyed sharing his love of sports, he never forced one sport, or sports in general, on David. He pushed only school, not sports. He wasn't dreaming of his sons becoming professional athletes. He spent less time playing basketball with his sons than he did playing many other sports.

And look what happened: David and Chuck both became college basketball players, and David became the MVP of the NBA.

You never would have guessed it, though, when David was in ninth grade.

*   *   *

Every day David practiced with the middle school basketball team. David watched every game. He played only if the game was a blowout. He was 5'9" and a good athlete. But he'd never practiced or played pickup games for hours on end, as so many other kids had, so he didn't have their moves or their sure shots.

Not playing frustrated him. He had never quit anything in his life. He knew his parents didn't want quitters in their family. They believed when the going gets tough, the tough get going. They believed in a never-say-die attitude. They preached all those old sayings, and David believed in them.

David debated a long time. He didn't want to be a quitter, but why waste his time when he could be studying or doing something else?

Finally, he went to his father and said he wanted to quit.

"Dad," he explained, "I'm not getting any playing time. The only time they put me in is when we're twenty points up and there's two minutes left. It doesn't make sense for me to play."

His dad had gone to the games. He knew the score. He thought his son was a little better than the coach did, but he didn't think parents should tell coaches what to do.

They talked about David's reasons. If David were playing a lot and wanted to quit simply because he wasn't doing well, that would have been different. But he wasn't playing and wasn't having fun, and if he'd rather study than shoot hoops, why, Dad wasn't going to argue. The conversation lasted all of one or two minutes.

"Fine," Mr. Robinson told David. "You don't have to play."

Then David went to tell his mom.

"David," she asked, "are you quitting because you're embarrassed not to be playing?"

"No," he said, "I feel my talent is being wasted. I don't want to be a bench warmer. I feel it's a waste of my time."

If he had wanted to quit because the coach upset or intimidated him, Mrs. Robinson would have suggested he explain his feelings to the coach first. But this answer satisfied her. If he wanted to quit something really important, like school, that would have been different.

"To be a quitter is to be a loser," his mom told David. "But sometimes you need to quit something. You have to be very level-headed about it. It's a thin line between quitting something and being a quitter in life. If you can recognize the line that says, 'Quit now while you're ahead,' you'll be okay."

David said, "I can always make a team in any sport, but I don't just want to make the team. I want to play."

7

The Electronics Genius

David didn't miss basketball. He simply dove into other interests.

When he was fifteen, he put together a wide-screen TV from a kit all by himself. Even though he wasn't supposed to.

Mr. Robinson had bought the Heathkit and left all the loose parts in a big box in the den. When he came back from two or three weeks at sea, he and David would work on it together.

David was supposed to wait until his dad got home. But the anticipation was too much for him.

It was summer time and he didn't have any school, and it was killing him to see that TV sitting there in the box. So one day when his mom was at work, he started putting the kit together without telling anyone.

When his sister saw what he was doing, she was horrified. She tried to get him to stop, but he wouldn't listen to her. As soon as their mom got home from work, Kimberly ran outside and met her at the car.

"Mom!" she yelled. "I tried to stop him! David is in big trouble!"

"What happened?" Mrs. Robinson asked.

"He went into that box, and he's messing with daddy's television," Kimberly said.

"He and his daddy will build it when his daddy gets back," Mrs. Robinson said.

"No, Mom, you don't understand," Kimberly said. "He's got a whole board done."

Mrs. Robinson hurried inside, and there was David, putting the pieces together with a soldering gun, a tool that melts metal parts and glues them together.

If he made a mistake, David could ruin a very expensive kit.

"David," his mom said, "do you know how much that kit cost?"

It was something like $500 or $600.

"But, Mom," David protested, "I know what I'm doing."

And he kept on working while his mother stared in disbelief.

"Your daddy is going to kill you," she said.

"I'll take the responsibility," he said.

"You better not solder on that board unless you're absolutely sure because it will be ruined if you're wrong," she said.

"Mom," David replied, "you worry too much."

David wasn't one to talk back to his mom. He convinced her he knew what he was doing. He said he was being very careful to read the directions and check everything two or three times before he soldered anything together.

So she let him continue, and after a while, he had everything together.

"I'm finished," he told his mom. "I'm just waiting for Daddy to come back, and then we can light it off."

Still, Mrs. Robinson was sure her husband would be upset when he came home and found out what David had done. So when his ship came back and she had to drive over to pick him up, she was nervous and afraid of what he was going to say.

"Honey, don't get mad," she said, "but David put your kit together."

"Oh," he said, "I wouldn't worry about it. He knows what he's doing."

His answer surprised her. But she was still worried.

"But do you know how much that thing cost?" she asked.

Mr. Robinson nodded his head. Of course he knew! He had paid for it, and it was a lot of money for anybody, but especially for a middle-class family in the early eighties. When he got home, he checked over the TV very, very carefully, asking David all sorts of questions.

Finally, he was convinced. "It looks okay," he said.

David said he thought so, too, except one piece was missing. He said it hadn't been included in the kit. Mr. Robinson checked to see if David had put the piece in the wrong place. After he was convinced David had done everything right, they drove to the Heathkit store and told the manager what had happened.

"*He* put it together?" the manager said, not really believing that anyone as young as David would be smart enough and handy enough to handle such a complicated job.

David convinced the manager when he looked at a nearby floor model and started telling the technician what the problem was. The technician made the changes David suggested—and then it worked nicely. The Robinsons got their missing piece, went back home, put it in, and the TV worked perfectly. The picture was sharper than Mr. Robinson had seen on any other six-foot screen. And David put it together so well, it still can be found in the Robinsons' old home in Woodbridge, Virginia, nearly fifteen years later.

8

A Star Is Born

After quitting basketball in ninth grade, David didn't play again until he was a senior—and then only because of homesickness.

When the Robinsons moved to Woodbridge, Virginia, on Halloween in 1982, David remained in Virginia Beach, 185 miles away. He stayed with a friend's family. His dad thought he'd want to be with his friends in his senior year in one of the nation's best schools.

David was too obedient to object.

But every morning, he woke up early and called his mom before he left for school. Every day he had a different excuse for calling.

This went on for about a week straight. Finally, his godmother told his mother, "Freda, David has called every day. He's homesick. He's lonesome. He's not calling because he needs money. Ask him if he wants to come live with you."

The next morning, David called again.

"Mom, whatcha doing?" he asked.

"David," his mom said, "you've called me every day. Do you want to come up here?"

She barely got the question out of her mouth.

"Yes, ma'am," David said, quick as could be.

Mrs. Robinson had never wanted to leave her son behind. She'd cried the night they left without him. Now she started crying again, thinking how sad her son must have been while separated from his family. She called her husband, who was already at work, and told him.

"Why are you calling me? Get in the car and go get him," Mr. Robinson said.

Mrs. Robinson hung up the phone and called David right back.

"I'll be down there in three hours," she said. "Tell the guidance counselor I said to get all your papers together because you're moving."

"Oh, yes, ma'am," David said, and his mom could hear the happiness in his voice. She raced to Virginia Beach and found him with his bags packed and his paperwork complete.

"Mama," he said, "I'm so glad you came. I missed you."

They got home and unpacked. The next morning Mr. Robinson took David to the big high school a few blocks away. But when they got to Garfield High, they were told David was supposed to go to Osbourne Park High. It seemed silly because Osbourne Park was thirteen miles and a half-hour bus ride away. But it turned out to be a blessing.

Garfield High was bigger, with a rougher crowd of teens and such a good basketball team, David probably wouldn't have played much there.

Osbourne Park was a good school, with a basketball team that could use another tall guy. When David showed up, he was sent to a guidance counselor who doubled as the varsity basketball coach. Art Payne took one look at this skinny 6'7" senior and asked him to try out for the team. David said he would. For the rest of the day, other kids kept coming up to him and saying, "You've got to play basketball; you've got to play basketball." Everyone was so enthusiastic, he couldn't say no.

The team already had been practicing for about a week, and that afternoon, David watched the workout and took a few shots in his stocking feet. He passed his physical that night and started practicing the next day. Shortly thereafter, the starting center sprained an ankle, and David became a starter, mostly because he was tall and athletic. He didn't really know what he was doing, didn't have the moves that other kids had, and didn't have the muscle to compete with stronger, more aggressive players. David would play well for a few minutes, and then his mind would wander and he'd sleepwalk for a few minutes.

Coach Payne could tell David's heart was not really into it, but he was understanding and didn't push too hard. He brought in a former college center to help David learn the basics of playing near the basket. David averaged about fourteen points a game and was voted to the All-Metro second team, All-Area, and All-District teams.

He actually did better in baseball than he did in basketball. He'd stand on the pitching mound and tower over hitters, scaring them with his height and his fastball's heat.

But he wasn't the most accomplished high school athlete in the family. Kimberly had played two years of varsity tennis. Chuck qualified for the state meet in two track events, made the all-city basketball team as a junior, and averaged more than twenty points a game as a senior.

All David wanted out of sports was a college scholarship. He didn't think he had a future in sports. Nobody did.

Only a dreamer could have predicted he would become an All-American in three years, College Player of the Year in four years, and NBA Rookie of the Year in six years.

9

You're in the Navy Now

It was time for the most important decision any teen will make: choosing a college. David wanted to go to a military school with a good engineering department. Basketball did not matter very much to him. But his basketball ability brought him a few scholarship offers and so did his amazing score of 1320 out of 1600 on the SATs. David could go just about anywhere he wanted. His choices quickly narrowed down to Virginia Military Institute and the Naval Academy.

David and his dad visited VMI, and Mr. Robinson liked the small campus and the basketball coaches. He thought that if David kept growing and developing, maybe he had an outside shot at the NBA. VMI graduates could go straight to the NBA or another good-paying job, whereas the Naval Academy forced graduates to serve the next five years in the military. Mr. Robinson didn't want David tied down, so he favored VMI.

But David came back from a weekend at the Naval Academy dreaming about engineering labs, not dollar signs.

"Mom," he said, "the equipment there is great. But I just can't make up my mind."

His mom knew why he couldn't make up his mind. David didn't want to hurt anyone's feelings.

"David," she said, "I like the Naval Academy, but what do *you* like?"

"Dad likes VMI," he replied.

"David," she said, "Go where *you* want to go. Keep in mind which is the best school for you, not where I want you to go or where your daddy wants you to go."

"Mom," he said, "I know the best school already, and that's the Naval Academy. Mom, you should see that lab."

But David was an obedient son who didn't want to disappoint his dad. When Dad pressed for an answer, he heard—or thought he heard—David say, "Yes, I guess I'll go to VMI."

And so Mr. Robinson called VMI, and three

recruiters drove 120 miles to sign the skinny, raw basketball recruit.

The VMI recruiters were in the den, talking to
David and his dad, when Mrs. Robinson walked down
the stairs and into the room.

"Who are these people?" she asked.

"These are the people from VMI coming to sign
David," Mr. Robinson said.

"No, they're not!" Mrs. Robinson said.

The recruiters and father were surprised. They
thought the matter was settled. Now, Mrs. Robinson
had raised doubt. Everyone turned to look at David.

"David," his dad asked, "have you made your
mind up yet?"

The coaches and parents waited for what seemed
to be an unbearably long time. They didn't know what
David would say.

"I'm going to the Naval Academy," he said, and
he thanked them for coming.

Disappointed, the VMI coaches left.

Mrs. Robinson asked her son, "You're not going
because I liked it, are you?"

"Mom," he said, "this is the best place for me."

"Be sure you're going there for the right reasons," she said.

"I am," he said.

Mrs. Robinson felt like dancing, but she didn't
because she knew she had to cheer up her husband.

"The education will far outweigh five years of quick money, and basketball is secondary," she told him.

"I guess you're right," Mr. Robinson said, quietly.

He was a little disappointed and embarrassed. But he knew the final decision was David's, not his. If David wasn't happy in college, he might not work and study as hard as he should. And a lot of work lay ahead—as he learned that very first day at Navy.

That was David's longest day ever.

In the morning, he got sworn in.

In the evening, he got swore at.

All day and all night he got bossed around as if he were a common criminal.

"What have I gotten myself into?" he asked himself, and sleep did not come easy that night.

And then he was required to swim one hundred meters.

Four laps. He couldn't make it.

David thought about quitting. He didn't know if he could handle the hazing and rigorous physical conditioning that the plebes, or freshmen, had to endure to prove they were tough enough to become Navy officers. But the lessons his parents taught him came back to him. He decided to stick it out.

It wasn't easy. David's college courses included thermodynamics, navigation, advanced calculus, physics, computer science, electrical engineering, weapons, history of science and technology, contemporary American literature, advanced programming, celestial navigation, advanced numerical analysis, computer data structures, partial differential equation, and economic geography.

Marching early in the morning. Classes most of the day. Basketball practice every afternoon. Basketball games and trips at night and on the weekend. And then there was the homework. He thought it came in two forms: too much and way too much.

David got so tired he kept falling asleep while sitting in class. He even slept standing up. It got so bad, the Naval Academy officials thought he had a medical problem. They learned the real problem when he broke his hand while boxing in physical education class. X-rays of the broken hand showed a gap in his bones, meaning they were still growing. In fact, he was growing so fast, his body needed extra rest to keep up. That's why he was sleeping all the time.

The news of the broken bone didn't disappoint the Navy basketball coaches and doctors. In fact, it did just the opposite. The doctor was excited when he called Mrs. Robinson with the news.

"David will probably be a seven-footer," he said.

This was amazing news for the Midshipmen. Because of the close quarters on its ships and submarines, Navy wanted most of its students to be shorter than 6'6". A certain percentage of each incoming class could be as tall as 6'8" but no taller. David was 6'7½" when he took his physical and was accepted in

February 1983. Once accepted, Midshipmen cannot be kicked out if they grow. And grow David did. He was 6'9" by the time he entered the Academy's conditioning program in May and 6'10" by the end of his first year.

The coaches had thought David could become a decent small forward. Now, realizing how tall he would grow, they were thrilled about the potential of a big-time center. With its height restriction and its five-year military commitment, Navy never had been able to sign enough great players to become a great team. Navy hadn't had an All-American basketball player since 1933. It hadn't been good enough to go to the NCAA tournament since 1966.

David Robinson could change all that.

10

Stay or Go?

David missed the first four games of Navy's 1983–84 season while his broken hand healed. When he finally made his college debut, hardly anyone noticed.

He didn't score a point.

He grabbed just one rebound.

They don't write books or make movies out of games like that. David was 6'9" and a skinny 185 pounds. He didn't really know what he was doing, and he didn't seem to care. He would sit in math class during sixth period and say to himself, Oh, brother, I have to go to basketball practice today.

But his feet and brains were quick. He learned

58

from Coach Paul Evans, who screamed and pushed him every day. He learned from the starter ahead of him. Cliff Maurer was big, strong, and clumsy, but he showed David how to fight for rebounds and how to make a variety of big-man moves. David averaged 7.6 points and 4.0 rebounds a game and was voted ECAC South Rookie of the Year.

Coach Evans tried every trick he could think of to motivate his prize pupil. He even asked David's dad for advice. Finally, he called David into his office and told him he could make a lot of money in the pros if he worked to develop his game. David wasn't convinced. He still thought basketball was just a small part of his life. But he worked with Navy's strength coach and put on twenty-five or thirty pounds of muscle. And he spent the summer playing against college and pro players in the tough Washington Urban Coalition League.

He came back to Navy as a 6'11" sophomore starter, but he still wasn't anything special until the Midshipmen went to Carbondale, Illinois, for a holiday tournament called the Saluki Shootout. In the first game against Southern Illinois and its 6'11" center, David was devastating. He scored thirty-one points and grabbed thirteen rebounds. In the next game against Western Illinois, he was even better. He scored thirty-seven points and pulled down seventeen rebounds. He was too quick for big men to cover and too tall for the little guys. He beat the little guys down

the floor on the fast break and outjumped the big guys for rebounds and dunks.

All the local papers bragged about him. Even *Sports Illustrated* noticed, naming him Player of the Week. College experts started calling him one of the nation's best big men. And for the first time, David started thinking maybe he really did have a future in this game.

He finished the season averaging 23.6 points, 11.6 rebounds, and 4.0 blocked shots a game. He led Navy to its first NCAA tournament since the sixties. He helped the Midshipmen beat favored Louisiana State in the first round before losing a close game to the Len Bias-led Maryland Terrapins.

By season's end, he was 7'1" and a true pro prospect. He faced a big decision. Students could leave the Naval Academy after two years and face no future military obligation. But if they came back for a third year, they were expected to graduate and spend five seasons in the military. Should David return to Navy and risk delaying—or even destroying—an NBA career? Or should he transfer to a big basketball school, work on his game, and try to improve his basketball potential and earnings?

He debated the pros and cons with his parents many times over the course of several months. The Naval Academy superintendent suggested David might not have to serve all five years but offered no written guarantees. He hinted that David might not have to serve any time because he was so tall or maybe he'd serve two years but be allowed to play pro ball when he was off duty.

Transferring might be worth millions of dollars in just two or three years. But if he changed schools, NCAA rules would force him to sit out a season, and no one could guarantee he'd play once he was eligible.

His father told him to think about his career after basketball. His mother told him to remember the commitment he had made to Navy. She said it was just like the chores he had as a child. He had a responsibility to fulfill his obligation.

He thought, Where will I go? Would I be comfortable? Would I play center? What if I transfer somewhere and then a hotshot shows up? If I stay at Navy, at the worst, I'll have a great education and in five years, I'll still be 7'1".

David chose academics ahead of basketball. He showed his loyalty to Navy and was praised for choosing to serve his country instead of letting the almighty dollar rule his life.

The Admiral Takes Command

David couldn't stop sweating. He was in Spain, but he felt as though he were in an oven. It was 105 degrees, and yet his United States' teammates were working furiously while competing in an international event called the Jones Cup in the summer of 1985.

They motivated him to push himself harder than he ever had in basketball. But when he returned to Navy and faced lesser competition, he relaxed just as he had when he was getting good grades in school. Why kill himself when he was already the best?

With their stern but polite pressure, his parents

had usually coaxed him out of his laziness. But when Coach Evans tried to push him, David rebelled. Coach was an old-fashioned screamer like Indiana's Bobby Knight or Ohio State's Woody Hayes. Seldom was heard an encouraging word. Often was heard a curse word. Navy's coach could swear like a sailor.

One day Coach thought David was sloughing off in practice.

"Get out of the gym!" he yelled, and pointed to the door. He was kicking his star out of practice!

David walked out, more mad than motivated. Evans is playing mind games to motivate me, he thought. That may work with other guys, but not me.

David decided to tune out his coach. He even threatened to quit the team.

"Hey, man," David told Coach Evans, "you're being a jerk."

He wanted to enjoy basketball as just one of his many interests. "Basketball," he told his dad, "is just something else to do, another part of life."

And yet, as much as he disliked Coach Evans' methods, they did motivate him. I'll show him, David thought, and he did.

As a junior in 1985–86, he averaged 22.7 points and led the nation with 13.0 rebounds and 5.9 blocks a game. He set NCAA records for blocks in a game, season, and career. He was named an All-American by just about every organization except The Associated Press and United Press International. He was such a commanding presence for Navy, he was dubbed The Admiral and The Aircraft Carrier.

He led Navy to its second straight NCAA tournament. The Midshipmen romped in the first round, but then they came up against Syracuse.

This was almost unfair. The Syracuse Orangemen were terrific. They had two future number one NBA draft picks in point guard Dwayne "Pearl" Washington and center Rony Seikaly. They were highly ranked and had beaten the Middies by twenty-two points earlier this year. They were playing on their home court with more than thirty thousand zanies screaming their fool heads off. And, to top it off, they tried to intimidate the Midshipmen by packing Navy's hotel with a wild St. Patrick's Day party.

Crazy fans filled the lobby and every part of the hotel. Everywhere David, his teammates, his parents, and his brother went, Syracuse fans mocked them.

"We aren't going to the game because Navy is a bunch of short hairs and can't beat Syracuse," some party-goers told them.

"We have already bought our airline tickets to the next round because there is no way Syracuse is going to lose to Navy," other fans told them.

On game day, the Carrier Dome was so packed, the crowd so loud, fans couldn't hear those next to them unless they screamed in each other's ears. The atmosphere was electric. The lead seesawed back and forth—until David took over.

He sliced inside for a basket and didn't pause to celebrate the way so many players do. He saw Pearl Washington racing downcourt, and he started chasing. Pearl had a lead on him, and he drove to the hoop better than any other guard in college basketball, but David ran him down, and just as Pearl tried to polish off his layup, number fifty swatted it away. David's momentum hurtled him past the end line and out of bounds. Syracuse's Wendell Alexis grabbed the loose ball and went up with a shot. David climbed out of the crowd of photographers, leaped up in the air, and knocked down this shot, too. Navy tracked down the ball and raced downcourt. David flew down the middle and slammed home a thunderous dunk.

Navy never trailed again. David spanked Seikaly like a naughty child. Seikaly fouled out with four points and four rebounds. David scored thirty-five points, snared eleven rebounds, and rejected seven shots. When he left the game, even the *Syracuse* fans gave him a standing ovation.

The next game, the Middies won by one point after David scored with six seconds left. One more victory and they'd go to the Final Four. Alas, it was not to be. Duke was next, and the Blue Devils were ranked number one in the country for good reason. David scored twenty-three points, but the rest of the team could manage just twenty-seven, and Duke won easily.

*   *   *

David was a great success in his studies and his sport. He should have been truly happy, but he wasn't. He didn't know why. Is this all there is? he wondered. The creepy feeling bothered him that summer when he played in the World Championships in Amsterdam, Netherlands.

On the plane home, David and teammate Kenny Smith spoke with an evangelist about Christ. David prayed with him. But he didn't understand yet.

He had stopped going to church once he had gone away to college. He knew the Bible stories, but that's all they were to him: just stories. They didn't affect his life. They sounded good, but he didn't understand the true meaning of faith. He called himself a Christian, but Christ wasn't real to him. In the back of his mind, he knew there had to be more to this Christianity stuff, but he wasn't sure what. He didn't know how to get there. He didn't know if he were ready to get there.

*   *   *

Back at Navy, Coach Evans had left to join the University of Pittsburgh. He was replaced by his assistant, Pete Herrmann. David liked the more easy-going coach. He worked even harder and grew even better as a senior.

He led the nation again in blocked shots and ranked third in scoring and fourth in rebounding. He became the first college player to combine 2,500 career points with 1,300 rebounds and sixty percent shooting from the floor. He made every All-American team and all the major College Player of the Year awards. He set thirty-three Navy records and launched the Midshipmen to another NCAA playoff appearance.

This all made for great family fun. David's family put more than eighty thousand miles on their 1979 Pontiac Bonneville, most of them to watch his games and even many of his practices. The big old boat of a car bore the license plate NA50VY, signifying their son wore number fifty and played center for Navy. His family grabbed seats close to the floor, and his little brother did back flips out of the second row whenever David dunked, which was often.

David's college career had not begun in storybook fashion, but it ended that way. The Midshipmen traveled to the NCAA East Regional in Charlotte, North Carolina, where they were to open with the highly ranked Michigan Wolverines. Fifteen minutes before the game, when players and coaches usually have tunnel vision, David again displayed his active mind and his many activities.

He turned to Coach Herrmann and asked, "Coach, have you ever tried tae kwon do?"

Coach was shocked. "What?" he asked.

"I'm into it now and it's great," David replied. "It really helps me a lot."

Tae kwon do is a martial art similar to karate. David then went out and chopped through the Wolverine defenders as if he were a black belt and they were papier-mache.

The fans stood and clapped when it was announced during the game that David had just won the Naismith Award as College Player of the Year. And then he really gave them something to cheer about.

Number fifty scored fifty points, a career high. He dazzled everyone with his assortment of dunks and drives, spin moves and jump shots. The Midshipmen were no match for Michigan's superior athletes and lost by fifteen points, but that didn't diminish David in anyone's eyes.

Coach Herrmann took David out of the game with two seconds left just in case anyone wanted to applaud David's effort. Everyone did. The fans' standing ovation was long and loud. One by one, Michigan players ran over to shake his hand. His Navy teammates jumped off their chairs and bear hugged him.

The applause lasted for several minutes.

David put his hand over his heart and sang "Navy Blue and Gold" with his fellow Midshipmen.

"No matter where I go or what I do," he told them, "I'll never forget you."

His spectacular college career was over.

12

San Antonio's Savior?

It was May 20, 1987. Graduation day at the Naval Academy. David and 1,021 fellow graduates and their families and friends gathered in Halsey Field House, home of so many of David's heroics the past four years.

One by one, each of the thirty-six Navy companies walked to the podium. As the twentieth company marched toward the stage, a professor walked over and asked David for an autograph. David rolled his eyes. The star center didn't want to be the center of attention. The line shuffled forward, and finally, it was David's turn. He shook hands and received his mathematics diploma from George Bush, the vice president and future president of the United States.

When the last midshipman had received his degree, the graduates shouted "Beat Army!" and threw their hats in the air.

Then the most famous graduate of the Class of '87 was named an ensign and assigned to the new submarine base in Kings Bay, Georgia. The new Secretary of the Navy ruled David didn't have to serve the normal five-year commission because he was too tall for ships, submarines, and planes. But he did have to spend two years in Georgia before he could join the NBA.

Three days later, the San Antonio Spurs won the NBA draft lottery and the first choice in the June draft. They could choose anyone in the country. Did they dare draft David? Yes, he was a great college player. But the Spurs were in such sad shape that the owners might be forced to sell the team or move it before David was allowed to play.

Plus, there was no guarantee they could even sign David. Because he couldn't play the next two years, he had more choices than the average NBA prospect. He could sign with the Spurs, or wait until the 1988 draft and let some other team draft him. If he didn't like the second team, he could turn down its offer, and, just when his Naval duty ended, he would be free to sign with any team in the league. He was one of those "franchise" centers who arrive maybe once or twice a decade. He could let all the NBA teams fall all over themselves throwing money at him and then pick his favorite city, team, and contract. Even in the multi-million dollar world of the NBA, he was in a dream bargaining position.

Still, the Spurs said they planned to draft David in June, and they did.

David and his family didn't make any promises. San Antonio would have to prove it wanted them, and the Spurs and the city set about doing so.

David didn't make his first visit to San Antonio until September, and the greeting was something out of a storybook.

San Antonio is one of the nation's largest cities, but the Spurs were the only pro sport in town. They meant everything to the local sports fans and politicians. The mayor wanted to build a domed stadium in hopes of keeping the Spurs and gaining an NFL franchise, but the prospects were dismal unless The Admiral landed. The Spurs weren't winning, they weren't drawing good crowds, and they weren't going to be staying in San Antonio much longer if they didn't turn around in a hurry.

David didn't want a royal greeting, but with so much at stake, how could San Antonio do otherwise?

The Spurs spent $16,000 just to charter a private jet that picked up Ambrose, Freda, and Chuck

Robinson and David's two agents in Washington, D.C. They flew to Jacksonville, Florida, to pick up David.

When they landed in San Antonio, they were greeted by seven hundred screaming fans, the Chamber of Commerce Red Carpet Welcoming Committee, and the DeCampanis Mariachi Band. Rain had been forecast, but as if by omen, the skies turned blue and the sun popped out. They walked across the red carpet as the band played "Anchors Aweigh." The fans chanted "David! David! David!" and waved signs with messages such as "Say Yes, David" and "Pretty Please." A state senator made The Admiral an honorary admiral in the Texas State Navy. David said a few words to the fans, went inside to talk with the media, and then was whisked to his hotel in a fancy limousine.

The Robinsons didn't get just any old hotel room. They got the biggest suites in the nicest hotel in town. They had a bedroom, a dining room, and a living room with a fireplace. They had flowers and jumbo shrimp too.

They went downstairs to a fancy dinner with a group of Spurs players, coaches, and front-office people. After dinner, the players took David to the city's best night clubs. The next morning, the mayor and the Spurs' bosses gave the family a helicopter tour of the city. Their two helicopters landed right on the grounds of the city's nicest country club, and they ate lunch and played a round of golf. Then came time for a private dinner at a fancy French restaurant and a

ferry ride down the San Antonio River and its famed Riverwalk.

The next day, they met with Spurs' management one last time. They made no promises, but on the flight home, they talked about their impressions.

They had never been to San Antonio before. David's dad thought he'd find tumbleweeds and prairie grass. He was impressed by the beautiful greenery, the warm weather, and the warm reception from the city, fans, and team. David's mom thought the Spurs had put on the perfect weekend.

San Antonio reminded David of Navy. He saw room for growth on this young team, just like Navy. The team would be built around him, rather than forcing him to sit on the bench a couple of years as he learned the game. And he liked the Spurs' dedication, the city's enthusiasm, and the comfortable small-town feel of the big city.

Still, he thought about other pro possibilities until November when he told his agents to go ahead and see what kind of contract the Spurs would offer. The negotiations were quick as a hiccup. His agents asked, and the Spurs gave. The deal made David the richest basketball player in history and the richest sailor since Blackbeard. It covered ten years—two in the Navy and eight pro seasons—and was worth $26 million, an incredible figure that would grow even bigger before it was through.

David had come from a middle-class family. Suddenly, he was rich beyond his wildest dreams.

First, though, it was back to Georgia and his desk job and reality. As a civil engineer, he oversaw the construction at Kings Bay's explosive handling wharf. Nuclear missiles would be loaded from this pier onto Trident submarines. But this job wasn't dangerous unless you count the time David dropped a pencil sharpener on his foot.

This job also didn't give him much of a chance to work out, let alone compete against top-caliber basketball players. So David was rusty when he went to the 1988 Olympics Trials. He made the team because of his reputation, but Coach John Thompson wasn't happy with his performance, and David wasn't very happy with the way the Georgetown coach used him. David averaged only 12.8 points and 6.8 rebounds a game during the Olympics.

He didn't knock Coach Thompson publicly, but plenty of sports writers and sportscasters did. Coach was condemned for a multitude of mistakes. He had taken too many defenders and personal favorites and too few three-point shooters. He made great players fit into his Georgetown system, rather than making the system fit their skills. He substituted nonstop and broke momentum. He played Danny Manning instead of David in the final deciding minutes. Danny was shut out and out of position. David had nineteen points in twenty-six minutes but was powerless to prevent a defeat. What was supposed to be another automatic gold medal turned to bronze, and the whole country was angry.

Both the coach and the center had their reputations tarnished. Doubts were cast about how good David would be in the pros after yet another season away from the game. The critics wondered if David was simply too smart and too well-rounded a person to dedicate himself to basketball and become a fierce and determined star.

David wondered, too. He could not get the failure out of his mind. For the longest time, he blamed himself.

Would he really be San Antonio's savior?

13

Super Spur, Superstar

It was November 4, 1989. The long wait was finally over.

David Robinson was about to make his NBA debut.

And the San Antonio Spurs weren't facing just another ho-hum team.

They were facing the Los Angeles Lakers. David had sat beside his dad, watching on TV as the Lakers played for one championship after another. The Lakers had gone to the NBA Finals three years running and had won back-to-back titles. Famous Hollywood stars sat in the front row of the fabulous Forum to watch the Lakers' Showtime. The Lakers no longer had

Kareem Abdul-Jabbar, maybe the greatest center ever, but they still had James Worthy and A.C. Green and Byron Scott. And they had Magic Johnson, one of David's favorite players and maybe the greatest point guard in history.

Now San Antonio was going to see just how good David Robinson was going to be. Was he as good as so many people said? Was he worth all that money? Was he going to be rusty? Was he going to play as he had in the Olympics?

Since he had signed, the Spurs had won just 52 games and lost 112. They had changed owners and coaches and all but three players from the previous year's team. They were counting on David to change their sad standing.

David was the topic of conversation all over town. People talked about him as they strolled the Riverwalk or rode the tour boats up and down the San Antonio River. They talked about him at the Alamo, the old fort where Davy Crockett fought valiantly but vainly in 1836. They talked about him at the Rivercenter mall, where they could look across the street to HemisFair Arena. They talked about him on the military bases that circled the city.

David was normally calm as could be. But not this time, not under all this pressure. As he sat waiting in the locker room, he tapped his leg up and down, up and down, as fast as it could go. His stomach rumbled, and he felt sick. He ran to the rest room and threw up.

Finally, it was time for the national anthem, and he stood at attention, ramrod straight like a good Navy man. Then the game began, and his nervousness went away. Two minutes into the game, he caught a pass, leaped high into the air, and, with his back to the basket, slammed the ball over his head and through the net. The crowd went bonkers, and the Lakers, lacking Kareem, were overpowered inside.

Still, the Lakers ran off nine straight points late in the third quarter and seemed ready to tie the score with the Magic man leading the fast break. Down the lane he drove. Into the air he flew. Up the ball went. Down the ball went! David had come from nowhere to swat away the sure layup.

He was as good as advertised.

His first NBA blocked shot triggered a 6–0 Spurs spurt, and they never gave up the lead again. The Spurs, once pushovers, beat the Lakers, once champions, by eight points. They had arrived as a force in the NBA, and so had The Admiral.

He led the Spurs with twenty-three points. He led everyone with seventeen rebounds. He led Magic to say, "Some rookies are never really rookies. Robinson is one of them."

David and the Spurs were off and running. He was named to the All-Star team. He was named NBA

Rookie of the Year. He was even labeled the league's MVP by such fine coaches and players as Don Nelson and Charles Barkley. He helped the Spurs win thirty-five more games than the previous year. It was the greatest one-year turnaround in league history—better than the Celtics' thirty-two-game improvement with Larry Bird, better than the Bucks' twenty-nine-game improvement with Jabbar.

Then-Lakers coach Pat Riley compared him to Bill Russell, "only a better athlete." Center-turned-GM Wayne Embry compared him to Russell, only with "more offense." Center-turned-commentator Jim Chones predicted, "He's going to be the best center ever to play the game." Then-Phoenix coach Cotton Fitzsimmons said he surpassed Michael Jordan, Magic, and Bird as "the greatest impact player the league has seen since Jabbar." His own coach, Larry Brown, called him "the best player of that size I've ever seen."

The next year, David played even better. He led the league in rebounding, was the only player to rank in the top ten in four key categories, was named first-team All-NBA and All-Defense, and started in the All-Star Game. He won the IBM Award for the league's best statistical performance for the second straight year.

He had more money and fame and success than a man could dream about.

And yet something was missing.

14

Onward, Christian Father

David wasn't depressed, but he wasn't really happy, either. And that was peculiar because he had so much.

His job was a game, and he was great at it. He was a naval officer and a gentleman. He was tall and handsome and healthy. He had five fancy cars and two beautiful homes and everything he ever wanted to buy. He had a math degree from one of the nation's best colleges and anything he picked up, he could learn. He was an expert in computers and electronics and engineering. He played the piano and portable keyboards and saxophones and the guitar. He composed his own songs and jammed with Grover Washington and Branford Marsalis, his jazz heroes. He averaged in the 190s in bowling and in the eighties in golf. He even was a whiz in Ping-Pong and gymnastics. He flew first class and stayed in the most luxurious hotels in the country. He was pampered and praised everywhere he went.

"Can I carry your bag, sir?" the bellmen asked.

"Can I buy you a nice dinner, David?" the businessmen asked.

"You're the greatest," the fans said.

"I'll do anything for you," the gorgeous women said.

Chuck came to visit and marveled at his older brother's lifestyle. Everyone did.

"Boy, you've got it made," they said. "Man, oh, live, you should really be enjoying this. It's awesome."

And yet he wasn't really enjoying his life.

It's nice, very nice, he thought. But it's not satisfying. It's not fulfilling.

But he didn't understand why.

Not until June 8, 1991. The day he came face to face with God.

It began like any other day. A minister from a group called Champions for Christ had driven from Austin, Texas, to San Antonio to meet with the Spurs' front office. The minister happened to bump into David and a Christian teammate, Terry Cummings, and they talked casually for a while. Then the minister began to ask questions.

"David," he said, "do you love God?"

David was surprised. "Of course I love God," he said.

"How much time do you spend praying?" the minister asked.

"Every once in a while," David replied. "I eat three times a day, and I pray then."

"How much time do you spend reading your Bible?" the minister asked.

"There's one around here somewhere," David said, beginning to feel a little uneasy and ashamed. "I've got one. I just don't understand it. It doesn't make a lot of sense to me."

"When you love someone, don't you usually take time to get to know them? Don't you want to know them better?" the minister asked.

God is not a real person, David thought. But he didn't say it.

Christ was about to become real to him.

"The Old Testament says to set aside one day a week to honor God," the minister said. "When was the last time you spent one day, not one day a week but just one day to praise God and thank him for what you have?"

David swallowed hard. Finally, he understood why he felt so uneasy. He thought, I have never given God a day to pray and thank him. I feel like a spoiled brat. Everything is about me, me, me, me, me. How much money can I make? My life is all about David's praise and David's glory. Everybody cheering David. Everybody patting David on the back. I've never stopped to honor God for all he has done for me.

The realization hit him hard. He started crying, and he couldn't stop. He cried all afternoon. For the first time in his life, what someone told him about God really affected him. He decided the Lord must have sent that minister to deliver his message.

David started to think. Where am I going? What am I doing? Who am I as a man? What makes me any different than the next guy? Nothing, really.

It dawned on him: I can have all the material things in the world, but they mean nothing if my soul, my spiritual side, is empty.

He was scared. He thought, Without the Lord, I have nothing. All the money, everything I have— without him, I have nothing.

He closed his eyes and prayed.

"Everything you've given me," he told the Lord, "I'm giving back to you today."

That was the biggest moment in his life. It was the day he was saved. It was the day his whole life changed.

Unlike his prayers on the plane ride from Europe in 1986, this message was going to stick with him. When the minister left, he didn't forget. He dove into his Bible for the first time.

Six days later, the message hit home again when he watched the Chicago Bulls celebrating their first NBA championship. David watched Michael Jordan, the NBA's greatest player, hugging and kissing the NBA championship trophy and started wondering.

Is the trophy that important? Here I am with five cars, two houses, and more money than I ever thought I'd have. What more could I ask for? Where am I going? Here's Michael Jordan. He has more than me, and boy, I'd like to have some of the things he has. But is that almost a trap the world has set for me? Winning one trophy wouldn't be enough. Then you have to win five trophies. Then you have to go and do something else.

Twenty years from now, who really cares? Bill Russell has won eleven championships. That's really great; it really is. That's an unbelievable accomplishment. But how does that affect anyone else's life? It's over. It's gone. What did it change in a positive way? Bill Russell as a man might change people's lives in a positive way, but the things he accomplished mean far less than who he is as a man.

It all clicked. David realized, All I'm pursuing cannot fulfill me. I'm a successful athlete making a lot of money, but if I can't be happy with myself, something is wrong. Ninety-nine percent of the people in the world want to be in my shoes, but I'm still looking for more. Wake up! No matter how much you have, it's not enough because things can't satisfy your deepest needs.

I need the Lord!

As a kid, he'd gone to church only because his mother had made him. Christianity did not excite him. Now it did. Now it became the central point of his existence.

As he committed himself, he felt the Lord had blessed him in many ways. But he realized he had been spreading himself too thin. He was into everything: music, basketball, golf, all sorts of things. He dropped everything and studied the Bible, got into the Word and into fellowship with other believers. Because it was summer, it was easy to be immersed in the Word and surrounded by Christian friends who could build him up spiritually. He had plenty of time. For two months, the Lord blessed him with tons of knowledge and insight into life.

Then basketball practice resumed, and David was surrounded by people with wilder lifestyles. David had to be strong to avoid the temptations, but he was more than strong. He was on fire. He sought to get his team-mates and friends to understand that God was tapping them on the shoulder and telling them it was time to get right with him.

Faith changed his relationship with his family. His mother had been saved in 1983, and now they had even more to talk about. He had always been close to his brother, but when he first got saved and tried to share his sense of wonder, his brother didn't want to hear it. David wanted to talk about the Lord; Chuck wanted to talk about girls. But the more he watched and listened, Chuck saw how much happier David was, and soon, he gave himself to the Lord, too. So did his sister, Kimberly. Now, they enjoy a much deeper understanding of each other because of their relationship with the Lord.

Becoming a born-again Christian was also the turning point in David's love life. He had broken up with his long-time girlfriend, Valerie Hoggatt, and they didn't even talk with each other anymore.

When David first got saved, he told the Lord, "Don't put any women in my life." He didn't want to date anybody. He thought, Before I can learn to be committed to a woman, I have to learn to be committed to God. Following that, a commitment to a girlfriend and then a wife would be easy.

David didn't know it then, but Valerie had felt the same uneasiness while they were apart. She, too, had been searching for answers and had found them in the Lord.

They had been separated for nine months when the Lord led them back to each other. David thought he heard the Lord tell him, "This is the girl I've put in your life. Yours and Valerie's relationship before was without me, and it's typical for a worldly relationship to deteriorate like that, but with me, it'll be a whole new relationship."

And it was.

Just a few months later in December 1991, they were married. They had their first child, David Jr., in January 1993, and their second, Corey Matthew, in April 1995.

In God and family, David found the peace and satisfaction he couldn't get anywhere else.

He thought, I get fulfillment out of pleasing God, knowing I'm doing the things he's calling me to do. I get satisfaction in knowing God is smiling at me as a husband and father. When he sees me make an effort on the basketball floor, he knows I'm doing it for his glory. And he's pleased with that. As long as he's in control, I'm in good shape. I don't have to know what's coming in my future. I know it's going to be good. I don't have to worry about my kids' future. God gives me enough peace to know they may go astray for a while, but as long as I give them the basics, as long as I instill that love and passion and show them who God is, they'll come back. I'll spend time with them. I'll honor them as a father, and I know God smiles on me because I do that.

Serving the Lord became central in even the smallest things he did. For instance, he'd get up in the morning and change his son's dirty diaper to try to make life easier and better for his wife. He wanted to honor her. He wanted to thank God for a beautiful wife and two incredible kids.

His newfound faith also affected his NBA career.

From the moment he had first dunked a basketball, people had said he was too smart, too well-rounded to devote himself to be the absolute best basketball player he could be. Sour-faced fans and sports writers weren't the only ones saying it, either. Even his coaches, his teammates, and his dad wondered if he couldn't do more. He was even criticized for turning too nice once he became a born-again Christian.

Again, David turned to his faith for answers. He studied his Bible. He spoke with ministers and Christian friends. And he found more of a purpose and determination than he'd ever had.

This is what he realized: When I play for myself and my own glory, sometimes it's hard to be motivated because when do I have enough money? At what point do I have enough fame? How do I get over the little aches and pains? How do I find the motivation to get up and work out and push myself harder and harder and harder? Some people have that drive in them. But I never really have had that drive. If I can do things well enough for everybody's satisfaction, that's enough for me. Until people push me, I never go past that.

But now, God is giving me another reason to excel. He is giving me something beyond what anyone on earth has ever given me. God saw in me a perfection. If

I don't reach for that, I'm letting him down. I don't know what God has in store for me, but if I don't go get it, then I'm cheating God.

He thought about the conversation he would have with God when it was time to decide if he should go to heaven or hell.

"What did you do with the gifts I gave you?" God would say.

If he had not given everything he had, he would have to say, "I buried it in the ground."

No way do I want to say that to him, David decided. I have an unbelievable responsibility on the basketball floor to honor what God has given me. It's far more than what I have toward the fans, and it's far more than what I have toward the people who pay me or even to my teammates. I have a responsibility to go out on the floor and work to make myself better and better, not for my glory and honor, but for his. So that's my drive.

David decided God had given him special size and skills so that he could spread God's Word. The better David played, the more people would know him and the more they would listen to him. And the more people who knew and listened, the more people he could influence to become Christians.

So David began his crusade. He played harder. He chose to concentrate and compete every second he was on the basketball floor. He chose to lead more vocally, on and off the court.

In 1992, he led the league in blocked shots, was named Defensive Player of the Year, and led the United States to a gold medal in the Olympics. In 1993, he started in the All-Star Game for the third straight year. In 1994, he led the NBA in scoring. He scored an incredible seventy-one points in his final game to edge out the highly hyped Shaquille O'Neal for the scoring title.

"David is the best basketball player in the game," said John Lucas, his coach then. "He's the most talented and the most gifted. Shaquille O'Neal is a great player, but he isn't David. David plays all five positions and does all the things a point guard does. There has never been a player like him anywhere." And, said Seattle coach George Karl: "I don't think there's any question this is a different David Robinson than we've seen in the past. He's a much more dangerous player. I've always said the man, if he would ever commit to winning, would be as scary as anybody in the league."

David Robinson was about to get even scarier.

15

Role Model

David stared at the camera and snarled like a Doberman.

"Mr. Robinson doesn't like garbage in his shoes," he said. "If you're into drugs, don't come into my neighborhood. Mr. Robinson doesn't like garbage in his neighborhood."

He was selling shoes. But he was also selling an attitude. The Mr. Robinson's Neighborhood commercials—takeoffs on *Mr. Rogers' Neighborhood*—always offered messages for kids.

Another commercial featured his mother and Georgetown coach John Thompson.

"It's Coach Thompson and my mom with today's word. What's *stupid*?" David asked viewers.

"Not listening to Coach Thompson is stupid.

"Not listening to your mom is stupid.

"Dropping out of school is stupid.

"And," he concluded, his face practically jumping out of the TV, "always listen to your mom."

This wasn't just some phoney acting job. Maybe some athletes care only about themselves, but David cares about those less fortunate. And he dedicates his time and money to help them.

Even before he became a born-again Christian, he felt he should give something back to the community. Since being saved, David has been even more involved. He gives ten percent of his earnings to charity. In its first four years, The David Robinson Foundation donated more than one million dollars to charities, usually ones that help children and churches. It saved another million dollars to invest in charities in the future.

Some charities provide jackets and shoes for the cold weather. Some provide after-school programs. Some are youth camps with spiritual components. Others stress avoiding drugs, alcohol, and premature sex. David runs a Christmas Toy Drive every year, and as many as five thousand toys are given to needy children. Number fifty donates fifty tickets to every Spurs home game to children who've been nominated by their teachers for outstanding achievement.

David promised to give $2,000 college scholar-
ships to every member of the 1991 fifth-grade class at
Gates Elementary School in San Antonio. They come
from very poor families. They are mostly black and
Hispanic. But if they work hard enough to graduate
from high school, David will help them go to college.

He was nice, but he was also stern when he spoke
to them. "You better take it seriously and say to yourself, 'Man, I want to make something out of myself,'"
he warned his adopted class. He said he cared about
them so much, he was giving them enough money
that "I could buy me a nice Porsche."

The kids are ninth-graders now, and they gather
every month to discuss their progress. David shows up
and gives them pep talks and advice. Every year, he
takes them to a cookout and pool party at his parents'
home or a local amusement park.

David has paid for other kids' educations, and he
likes to speak to children in schools, churches, and
homes for the disadvantaged. If kids look up to him
because he's a star athlete, he doesn't mind. But he
also wants them to know he can do more than dunk a
basketball. He's also an excellent student, musician,
golfer, bowler, and computer expert. He couldn't have
done all that he's done if he hadn't studied hard and
learned a lot. He wouldn't have succeeded if he had
done drugs.

"I have the greatest job in the world, playing

basketball," he told one group of schoolchildren. "But there are also a lot of pressures, a lot of stresses. What do I face pressures with? Drugs? People know I have a lot of money, so they come to me and say, 'You wanna buy these drugs?' And I say, 'Nooooo, thank you. I don't want those things. Those things will mess me up for life. I won't be able to do the things I can do on the court.' And you guys won't be able to do the things you can with your life if you get caught up with drugs. I've seen a lot of guys who've had so many problems with drugs, and it hurts them so badly. It takes away a lot of your dreams, it really does. You can always recover from a mistake, but sometimes you can't repair the damage you do with drugs."

It used to bug David when he was constantly stopped for his autograph. It doesn't anymore because he uses it as a chance to spread his message. He signs his name, and just underneath, he adds a passage from the Bible. He tries to get a feel for the fan and give him a verse that will help him. Not every fan will go home and look up the Bible verse, but if only a few do, then maybe David has helped.

It's all part of spreading God's Word. David wants to touch as many people and reach as many lives as he can. David and his family think that's his calling. They think that's why God saved his life when he had those accidents as a baby. They always figured God left him

on earth for a reason. They didn't know what it was then. They think they do now.

"He reaches people because of basketball, but his purpose goes beyond basketball," David's dad said. "What he can accomplish with his ministry is more important than anything he can accomplish in basketball. He could be the next Billy Graham. I could foresee in five or ten years he could have numerous followers as in Billy Graham's crusades or the *700 Club*."

His mom feels the same.

"I don't know if he'll become the next Billy Graham," she said, "but I will say he is going to help a lot of people through his ministry. I think—I *know*—the Lord allowed David to live for a reason. He's chosen. I knew when David started breathing that day, I knew it could have only been the Lord. I knew there was a mission."

David knows now, too.

"When I became a born-again Christian," he said, "I learned that was God's calling for me. I have a responsibility to put it out on the floor every night and be the best I can be. This is the way I minister to people right now. People have watched me grow and change over the years. They've seen the difference in the way I've focused on the game and become more dedicated.

"When basketball is over, I'll be involved in some type of ministry. That's what the Lord has put in our hearts. I don't know what he wants me to do, but wherever he takes me, I'm going.

"I know God saved me for a reason. I've accomplished a lot in my basketball career now, but maybe there's so much more out there, it'll dwarf what I've accomplished."

16

Even MVPs Can Get Better

It was May 23, 1995. Bob Hill blinked back the tears as he told his San Antonio Spurs the news: David Robinson had just been named the NBA's Most Valuable Player.

He had coached David for less than a year, and grown men weren't supposed to cry, but Coach Hill thought so much of David the man, David the player, he couldn't help but choke up. The Spurs whooped and hollered and hugged and high-fived David.

He had won just about every award and honor there was, but this made it official: David Robinson was the best basketball player in the world. Only eighteen other men had ever been named the NBA's MVP. No other Spur had ever won it. Now David belonged in the same class of centers as Bill Russell, Wilt Chamberlain, Kareem Abdul-Jabbar, Moses Malone, and Hakeem Olajuwon. He could be mentioned in the same breath as Michael Jordan, Magic Johnson, Larry Bird, and Charles Barkley. Imagine it: He had beaten out Shaq, Shaquille O'Neal. He was more valuable than a Penny, Anfernee Hardaway. He was more dependable than a Mailman, Karl Malone.

The 7'1" center with the common name but uncommon game had topped Hakeem The Dream and Clyde The Glide Drexler and Sir Charles Barkley and Air Jordan and every other NBA nickname.

It was a dream come true—except David Robinson had never dreamed about this as a kid. He didn't have any sports heroes or hopes. He wanted to be an engineer or mathematician or surgeon. Instead, he had developed into a two-time All-American, a two-time Olympian, a six-time All-Star, and now an MVP.

He was thrilled. He thought back to the kid who wasn't good enough to play on his ninth-grade team. He thought back to the kid his sister called a nerdy brain child, more interested in science fiction than sports.

It's incredible how far I've come, he thought. I'm proud of this award because it shows I have grown as a player.

The next night was just as emotional. David had led the Spurs to the NBA's best regular season record and now the play-off semifinals. At halftime of their play-off game, the NBA held a ceremony at halfcourt.

Millions of fans from around the world watched on television. Nearly thirty-six thousand fans at San Antonio's Alamodome stood and applauded. NBA commissioner David Stern held the trophy in his arms, looked up at David, and said it was wonderful to give the MVP trophy to such a great player and person.

The top of the commissioner's head was about at David's shoulders. He reached up and handed David the trophy. It was a big, bronze sculpture of a basketball player with one leg off the ground, as if he were going up for a layup or dunk. David smiled and shook hands with the commissioner. He put the trophy in his left hand and lifted it over his head.

He closed his eyes and prayed to God. Thank you! Slowly, he circled around so everyone in the arena could admire it. He opened his eyes and the cameras flashed and the applause continued. He closed his eyes again and thought of a higher power. Then they handed him a microphone, and instead of telling the fans how wonderful he was, he told them how wonderful *they* were, and they roared some more.

But . . .

Even in the storybook world of the NBA, even for

the biggest and richest and most famous men, dreams
do not last forever.

The Spurs had already beaten the Denver
Nuggets and Los Angeles Lakers in the play-offs, and
now they were favored to win the Western Conference
championship. They were four wins away from the
NBA Finals and the dream matchup between The
Admiral and Shaq, the players voted 1–2 in the MVP
balloting. But first they had to get past the defending
champion Houston Rockets and the reigning MVP,
Hakeem The Dream Olajuwon.

The Dream became The Nigerian Nightmare for
The Admiral.

Hakeem drew David outside, faked one way, and
drove the opposite way. He backed in toward the basket and spun around to hit his famed turnaround
jumper. He even scored on a couple of 360-degree spin
moves and a no-look, over-the-shoulder shot that
looked like something only Air Jordan could do. He
scored thirty-one of his forty-one points after that halftime ceremony. David was outstanding himself, scoring thirty-two points, but he couldn't stop Hakeem,
and the Rockets won by ten points.

It went that way the whole series.

The Dream played like a dream. He averaged a
stunning 35.3 points, 12.5 rebounds, 5.0 assists, and
4.2 blocks a game. David's statistics were good for
most players—23.8 points, 11.3 rebounds, 2.7 assists,

2.1 blocks—but not for the MVP, not compared to Hakeem The Dream.

David missed a lot of shots, and couldn't stop Hakeem's shots. The Rockets won the best-of-seven series in six games and then swept Shaq's Orlando Magic to win the NBA title. People bragged about Hakeem and blamed David. But the critics couldn't make him feel any worse than he already did.

I've never felt this bad since I've been in sports, David thought. I feel as though I let my team down. It's just a crummy way to end a good year.

Just when David had seemed to reach the top, God reminded him he was human. Just when it seemed he was perfect and didn't have to work hard anymore, Hakeem had humbled him and shown him just how much more he had to do. He thought about it a long time and decided God was trying to tell him something.

He shared the lesson when he spoke to a group of kids over the summer. "God didn't say, 'David, we're going to make you lose in the play-offs and we're going to make Hakeem Olajuwon play great so you'll look like a clown.' He didn't say that to hurt my feelings, and he wasn't trying to hurt my feelings," David explained. "He was trying to say, 'David, you need to mature. You need to get stronger. You need to get better. So you can either cry about it or you can get better.'"

Even the best can get better. Even the best can

face tough times. But the way he responds is the measure of the man.

David decided to work harder than ever.

Basketball had always come easy to him. All the other good players had spent thousands of hours practicing and playing, but David always had been one of the best, and often *the* best without slaving away.

"Instead of doing all the things you do in the off-season, spend some time on the court and work on new moves," his dad told him many times. "Once you gain confidence in some new moves and develop some moves people don't know about, you're going to be awesome. I know you like to spend time with your family, and I don't have any problem with that, but if you're going to better yourself, you've got to practice."

David would listen and say, "Okay, Pops. You're right."

And then he would ignore his dad's advice and go off to his summer home in Aspen, Colorado. He'd go hiking in the Rocky Mountains and play with his kids and just generally goof off.

But this time was different.

This time, David listened.

"Failure doesn't get enough credit," David decided. "It teaches us humility, perseverance, and the value of hard work. When you fail, you have to learn from your mistakes and move on. God gives you challenges in your life, but he gives them to you for a reason. It's not like he's trying to hurt you or punish you. He's giving you those challenges so you'll grow up and mature."

David talked to Coach Hill about what he needed to do to improve, and when he returned in the fall, the coach could see the improvement. So could his buddy and teammate, Sean Elliott. "I think he worked harder than any summer he's ever had in this league," Sean said. "I saw him working in the gym before camp started, and before, you'd never see him."

The results were quickly obvious. By the start of 1996, David was first or second in the league in scoring, rebounding, and blocked shots.

"He did work harder this year," his dad said. "Perhaps it's because of maturity or the bitter taste of losing in the semifinals last year. Coach said he came back with some new moves he'd been working on over the summer. I know I've noticed the difference. I've seen a couple of new shots, and he's using his hook shot more. He used to use it once every six or seven games. Now, he might use it two or three times a game. Now, he has confidence in it."

Now, the Spurs are so thrilled they want David to remain a Spur for life. They gave him a brand-new contract that will pay him a big signing bonus plus $11.5 million every year until 2001.

Now, who knows what they might accomplish together? Michael Jordan didn't win a title until his seventh year, Hakeem Olajuwon until his tenth year,

Julius Erving until his twelfth year. Hakeem didn't play organized basketball until he was fifteen, and he's still getting better at age thirty-three. Why shouldn't David, who didn't play high school ball until seventeen, keep getting better at age thirty?

"That's the scary part: There's so much he still doesn't know," his dad said. "He's been in the league six full years and he's still learning. Looking where Hakeem came from versus where David came from, the two are very similar. Hakeem has three years on David. I still don't think David has reached his full potential."

David Robinson is the MVP and he's still working hard, still getting better. Now *that* ought to *really* scare the rest of the NBA.

YEAR-BY-YEAR STATISTICS

College stats (U.S. Naval Academy)

YEAR	G	FGM-FGA	PCT	FTM-FTA	PCT	REB	AST	BLK	PTS	PPG
83-84	28	86-138	.623	42-73	.575	111	6	37	214	7.6
84-85	32	302-469	.644	152-243	.626	370	19	128	756	23.6
85-86	35	294-484	.607	208-331	.628	455	24	207	796	22.7
86-87	32	350-592	.591	202-317	.617	378	33	144	903	28.2
TOTAL	127	1032-1683	.613	604-964	.627	1314	82	516	2669	21.0

Pro stats (San Antonio Spurs)

YEAR	G	FGM-FGA	PCT	FTM-FTA	PCT	REB	AST	BLK	PTS	PPG
89-90	82	690-1300	.531	613-837	.732	983	164	319	1993	24.3
90-91	82	754-1366	.552	592-777	.762	1063	208	320	2101	25.6
91-92	68	592-1074	.551	393-561	.701	829	181	305	1578	23.2
92-93	82	676-1348	.501	561-766	.732	956	301	264	1916	23.4
93-94	80	840-1658	.507	693-925	.749	855	381	265	2383	29.8
94-95	81	788-1487	.530	656-847	.774	877	236	262	2238	27.6
TOTAL	475	4340-8233	.527	3508-4713	.744	5563	1471	1735	12209	25.7

KEY: G games played, FGM field goals made, FGA field goals attempted, PCT percentage, FTM free throws made, FTA free throws attempted, REB rebounds, AST assists, BLK blocked shots, PTS points, PPG points per game.

DAVID ROBINSON'S WEB PAGE

Spurs Center David Robinson now has a web page on the Internet. The home page will lead you to a variety of items, including opportunities to join his fan club, correspond with his parents and the president of the fan club, and give patrons an opportunity to purchase NBA related merchandise through The Robinson Group, Inc.

It will also link you to some of our favorite web sites, including local TV stations, selected San Antonio web sites, and World Wide Web yellow pages.

To visit David's home page, use

URL HTTP://ourworld.compuserve.com/homepages/David Robinson_50

Some key words through various search engines are David; Robinson; Spurs; and Basketball.

For further information,

email 75352.2300@compuserve.com
or call Noel Hudspeth at 210-696-9639.